When Orchids Were Flowers

KATE KNAPP JOHNSON

DRAGON GATE, INC.
Seattle/Port Townsend
Washington

Acknowledgments

Grateful acknowledgment is made to the following publications in which some of these poems first appeared: *Ironwood*, "Letting Go"; *Northlands*, "Instructions to the Heart"; *Onset*, "Passing the Zero"; *Poetry*, "Anniversary" and "For Now"; *Quarry West*, "A Photograph Taken Just before the Birch Let Go" and "Your Circling"; *Sarah Lawrence Literary Review*, "Eben," "Your Love Poems," "Lines from a Small Death," and "This Other"; *Tendril*, "Red" (formerly entitled "Wanting You") and "James before Darkness"; World of Poetry Press, "You Were the Artist"; and *Wyvern Yare*, "Sometimes, Our Lives."

Especial thanks to Arthur Kornhaber, Jan Perkins, Thomas Lux, Douglas S. Phillips, and those members of the Sarah Lawrence community who have given freely their help and friendship.

Both the author and the publisher wish to express their gratitude to the Literature Program of the National Endowment for the Arts for a grant that helped support the publication of this book.

Dragon Gate, Inc., 508 Lincoln Street
Port Townsend, Washington 98368

Designed by Judy Petry.
Cover art: photograph © Mary Randlett, 1986.
        Orchids courtesy of Gary Baker, Baker & Chantry, Inc.

Library of Congress Cataloging-in-Publication Data

Johnson, Kate Knapp
        When orchids were flowers.

        I. Title.
PS3560.037954W5   1986   811'.54   86-13435
ISBN 0-937872-34-2
ISBN 0-937872-35-0 (pbk.)

*"It is all right
To tire of the earth.
To tire and go on working, head bowed."*
— THOMAS JOHNSON

for my mother and father

Contents

ONE

TWO

THREE

ONE ❧

"…*This touching
home goes far. This fishing in the air.*"
—LINDA GREGG

At dinner one night that early summer
we argued about Japanese dogwood, my father and I,
were they in bloom, was it too late in the year for the
                                     dogwood to bloom?
I tell you I saw them just today,
in the churchyard, trees of white blossom.
I tell you I broke a sprig of the dogwood,
I put that flower to my cheek just this day.
There was nothing to do but go to the churchyard, my father
                                         and I,
to see for ourselves, to settle this in the churchyard.
There in the falling light of the evening
when in the sky was just the first star,
there on the shadowy ground we stood
under the swell of three full trees.
There are the dogwood side by side in the midst of the
                                       churchyard,
rising over the numberless gravestones and markers.
We had come for argument's sake
to stand quiet
over the gray stone where my sister has lain all these years.
My father and I, there in the spell of evening shadow,
silent under the full-blossomed dogwood,
surprised for a moment to miss her after all these years,
still in the night grown suddenly dark,
still as the sky suddenly filled with numberless stars.

No sound lives in this house
but soft wheelchair sounds:
leather-breathings, wheels on a hollow ramp.
There's a slipper
that got caught in a spoke and fell off
a foot that couldn't notice,
a body that didn't speak.

By the bay window there's a piano
that can't be tuned, rocking chairs
that won't come forward again.
In the dining room the table has been set
on its end and the damp smell of tarpaulin
comes like real cloth into your lungs,
throat-strings,
until you're hoarse with it,
until it lifts itself
like a spoon to your eyes.

There's much that is sad in families.
This comes to us like a parachute
falling across our nights,
comes to us days
when our watches are set with anchors,
when our bellies uncork
and we simply slide down our intestines.
It comes — but it's not
so sad. Some nights we can play the white keys
with our tongues, and there's music
in our tunnels, music
in ivory.

1.
The implications of the hawk were clear enough:
first, that there is no
continuity, none at all, and the sky could end
tomorrow. And: that when the hawk aimed
he aimed for the split second
of the rabbit's afterthought, the initial glance
into death.

Now I am given a series of tests
like a child the teachers wonder about,
want to explore, question…
"Is there trouble at home?" "No,
no trouble at home…"
The tests are objective,
I am the thing watched and
watching. We note:

I throws itself from I
I doesn't like I
I doesn't get along with the other children
"Is there trouble at home?" No —
I simply doesn't like I
I gives I up

2.
Now comes the story of *them*.
She was a good cook. He
was extraordinarily handsome.
The first child died so they had some more;
these lived. She
was a very good cook, seldom
at home. He

pretended not to notice

how many centuries ago
she must have left him
in order to get so far away.
Neither of them said it mattered, "No,
not at all." I bleeds.
The blood does not fall to the ground
but into I's shoes. It is covert blood.
I noticed this just last year and was startled
but went on singing.
Into her shoes.

3.
No continuity? Yes, perhaps some:
he aimed in order to eat. He ate. These

are the implications of the hawk
which became clear
looking up at it: hunger
in ever-widening circles, white
at the edge of the fields of vision
beginning to make itself known

as the one congruity – I
was always the rabbit,
the thing surrendered.

The way it's snowing today —
nothing to do but stare out the windows, walk
from room into room.
The flakes aren't *falling* to the ground,
they are driven there. It was winters ago, snow
like this when the dun mare

kicked me in the chest and broke loose.
I told them at dinner she was gone. I told them
I didn't want to have to do
with the horses anymore. My father said, "Kate,
Kate, goddamn you," got up and went out looking for the mare.
She'd tangled herself in barbed wire down at the Canfield's pasture,
sliced through a tendon.
My father made me come out to see.
He said, "I want you to look at this mare
so that you know
what you've done.
I want you to put your hand to her."

I was scared of that horse
and then it seemed like just the beginning
of everything I was to be
afraid of. Now winter itself
can frighten me — months
of the driven white.
I've touched her, I know
what's been done.
But, Father, it keeps on snowing —
and we watch it,
watch it.
As if we had a choice.

To be stationed together in the same house
for nearly thirty-two years is no small trick.
Love has constantly
to be polished on the finger
and the children's drawings
dusted and hung by the icebox—
two figures of stick
holding hands on the lawn
while the chimney
gluts with smoke.

Out of her disaffection
or out of the consanguine willingness
to hurt, she turns to me, says
"I can't feel anything now.
When I try, I can't feel anything."
I am subsumed
by their marriage. I must feel
for both of them now,
reminding them to love each other, to love…

My father is proud of the years and waits
for more to pass. In this
he resembles the runner
who has forgotten the race but who runs on
to the next landmark anyway, and the next, the next.
He says, "She's my wife. Of course
I love her."
For their sake. I have told worse lies
for their sake.

The race is the artifice
that sets the runner in motion, the numb statutes
of marriage likewise
prod the couple on to bliss.

I have always believed that.
Thirty-two years is a recent miracle
and I prefer to stand here alone
burnishing their love
instead of fabricating my own.
There have been worse lies, I know.
For I'm the one who drew them
standing on the lawn,
the one who makes them hold hands in the picture
all year. All year long.

I can still draw her face
on air, so recently old,
just beginning to accept the telling
grays and lines, night coming in midmorning.

It was in the morning,
once, she put her face
against the cool glass while I was telling
a story to cheer her. But it was old,

not very funny. She turned too suddenly and said, "I'm
old."
That was all she ever said. One complaint. One morning.
That was all. And telling.
There are things it's best to face

privately. Once more I etch that sudden face
on the air with one finger, "I am old."
I am too. We're telling
the same ordinary story. Once, one morning

we tell it with our faces,
old and lined and, through the window, lit with morning.

In every emergency
I'm the one who makes the coffee.
It's ineffectual, all I can think of doing —
a small act, a meticulous sanity
that pins me back to the circumstances

of surviving. The Delft pitcher, cups
with their glued-on handles,
the oversized spoons. That's how it was
night after night when I hunched in my mother's kitchen

and waited for her to finish dying.
I wanted to be there.
I wanted to be anywhere else.
I made coffee.
I didn't know what I wanted…
Today, Andrew,
I receive news

of you. There's a certain mildness
in having it done with, that much I've seen.
I make coffee. I concentrate on this; it is the act

of touching my face in a mirror. I once believed
all forms of faith to be strictly
for the insipid. Today, I bring the cup close
and lean over it, thinking,
for now, for now.

"Perhaps I'll get used to hanging"
were not my grandmother's last words
but among them.

And mine, not so very funny after all,
stay in the air like bad bruises never healed,
stalling for time.

Here are the reasons I've never told you.
I've been locked in my house for years,
and the snow! Terrible,

the way dreams have limbs that stretch
so just when you think you've got hold of them
they walk away

as if there's no point anymore
in waking up and no one to tell you
if you did. But I'm getting used to doing and doing

without. I'm getting used to this house and to the trees
and the garden statue holding out his hand-
ful of winters.

The blue throat of my wrists
and the bright ring of chafing about my neck
are small inconveniences

my grandmother said one gets used to
before she put a piece of dry bread
like death in her mouth

and swallowed, taking unto herself
the birring of wings,
vicissitudes, the sheer luck

of departure.

I take my paints, my radio
to Riverside. I'm doing cranes and boats.
Now that winter's come
I'll have to do insides:
Trinity Church, still lifes,
Mother.

It was smaller there – no glass,
no belts, no cigarettes, fewer choices.
Now I want:
landscapes, stucco, mimosa, forests
of cowbane. But I don't know why:
why I was in, why
I'm out.

Mother watches me. She watches
like a widow. I think she is
a widow, a scarrow in the doorway.
She worries I'll try to do it again
and go back to the hospital, but they watch you there, too.
Only not like a widow, like something else;
lantern fish, wicked lighthouses.

I'm working with colors, using a black
so black it's almost red, I think,
the inside of a mouth when it's closed,
what's unseen, guessed.

"Ambivalent feelings about breathing."
I put this down as a sort of joke, a relief
to get it out,
to get all of this out.
I don't know about living.
Dying, I guess I'd miss some things;
I've always wanted to do marshes,

the bitterns. The sky

looks like a terrible snow
that I know is coming and will
be terrible – a premonition of falling backwards and nothing
to break that fall.
I should end this and go out.

Therapy – walking street after street.
Exercise – before the snows come.
But then again, why
stop here? Why
descend to the streets
when the streets will never be finished,
will never let me close off,
close off like this?

Mother
walks on the balcony. I burn
with the cold. It's an old trick, isn't it?
To say no one loves, no one cares.

My father has been placed
under the water.
There were no sutures for this
therefore the water.
Also: promises were made.
Also: tiny fingers at night
turning pages of salve.
You told me not
to let go of you like this
but when I get towards the last page
the promise seems different
and the water bright,
holding you supine,
refracted, where your face is all glister
and every bone
is missing.
And the reproach
missing. And the interment missing.
I put you there,
in the water, boatless —
so that the moon notices you
by coincidence,
so that its reflection
drops on you,
so that you are
the moon
of no planet I know
that's dying.

I've never believed
in the burial of your particular body
but see you instead
as something circling the sky, not

a star, but a space, some reservation
made in the night
which was not kept, a predictable light
gone out.

Vincible one, out-light of the sky,
my imagination will have you everywhere
where you are not. My imagination
even imagines itself

in grief. In truth
I am at a place prior
to all grieving, not having recognized
the familiar absences of myself

without you. Turning a pencil over in my hands
I am trying to identify
the hands — they are like something reflected
in a mirror reflected

in a mirror, your death that
remote, that endlessness
of emotion failing the heart
while the heart, failing too, just huddles under ribs.

From where I sit now I can see you.
My chin on the windowsill

is its own moon
and I have no use for any other

moon, which tonight, in illuminating, illumines only
the dark circling
the retina; light
having fallen away from the eye.

This is the only photograph I have of myself
that I'm not in.
The reason I'm not in it:
I'm in the house
which is just off
to the left, behind the branches.
The house is a kind of sanity
because the windows match,
because the roof deigns
to shrug and turn away,
insouciant, sure,
and all sanities are so.
The branches are birch.
The house is a willow.
I'm inside with my eyes closed
but you can tell
by the trembling leaves
willow from birch. And you can tell
by the way the birch is bent backwards
that its job is to hold
the willow.
Inside, I'm conifer —
my hands bear live cones.
And wind gazes like loss into my needles.
And wind lifts the emptiness of the willow.
And wind
tells the birch to let go.

The scene is complicated
because I have to play all three parts: myself,
Papa, and the orchids.
I stand in the white room watching Papa
come up the hill.
Of course, I *am*
Papa so the hill
has to come inside me a little.

After awhile, all I can see
is my own reflection in the window.
Above me, the orchids
pace in their attic,
always reaching the threshold before
Papa. This is the hard part
for although I wonder about that line
it can only be said one way
and there's a small death in it.

Later, I look out the window,
past myself, to the ocean.
The orchids are rowing away with Papa.
I call to them, "Come back! I will keep the night
from getting dark. I will make the lamps
bright inside."
When they don't answer I turn out the lights,
all the lights, and the scene ends.
It was better when Papa was here
to play his own part. It was better
when the orchids were flowers.

I carry my head down in token of mourning.
The dogwood has been hewn and carried off into the
woods.
　　Like a crippled woman she calls to all her children
　　but they cannot go to her.
Goodbye to the house where I grew up, where sunlight
　　came in all directions like the four white visions
　　of my parents' hands, lit birds.
Goodbye to the river we never named — it runs quick, wet in the wood
　　where the hewn dogwood calls in a voice the black fields
　　use at night, scarves falling around you.
Goodbye to the old gardens overgrown. I have basted the roots
　　of lilac and rose with dirt. I have lost my fingers
　　there in the dark earth. Goodbye
to the white book of prayer inscribed to me, marked
　　with the date long ago when I wailed in the minister's arms
　　and made vows of childhood, goodbye.
The clapboard church is empty on the common. Once
　　between its palms it held the face of its bride. Now
　　is the day of leaving.
Goodbye my mother, my father.
Goodbye, what I have to learn I learn alone, as you before me.
Goodbye to the dogwood, last and faithful lover calling.
I make my tears. There is wind under my knuckles.
And prayer.

If I could say anything now
I would want you to understand
the part about the field.
How it was simple. How I died upon entering
the field. Like walking into a clearing, or
into a cage. I took to it like air, that death.
And how it was simple.

But there are other things too. I would tell you
ashes
falling in the kitchen. We consumed everything.
We folded the napkins politely
so there would be nothing
left, and
nothing left out. The courtesy of it!
The square shape of napkins, little diplomas
of cuisine life. But
how nothing was left.

I would also tell you the importance of touching
that constellation. Saying
After love the pain is what's final. And saying
After pain is lived for a long time
the stars begin to come back, retrieving
their holes in the sky, traveling
in small groups. One night by the dogwood tree

I threw my hands up into the air, glad
with their uselessness.
I touched Orion. I touched him.
How far up into the sky
I fell that night.
And it was like entering a field
in which nothing has been left out,
not the gold, not the ashes.

And how it was simple,
like breaking
from darkness into a clearing. Like breaking
from darkness.

TWO

you speak of the window

as if it lies between you,
as if you stand looking through it
from some room just under the eaves
watching the sea, watching
for your own blue boat
to appear on the water

that never appears.

In this letter what you point to
you're pointing beyond. You mention standing
in front of a shop looking in at cut
iris and phlox,
lupin and not buying anything
but the reflection of your own hands
in the glass, two salted fish staring and airless.

This letter keeps disappearing.

Or you do.
You keep going behind the mirror
and returning without understanding
who's back there.
You say sometimes you feel like a jackal
in the desert, and so hungry
you'd like to burn down the night.
But I'm not so sure.

I think you like
the distance of water.
I think you put that window there on purpose

because you're afraid of the sea,
because you're afraid

the blue boat is real.
And out in the wind.
And rocking.
Rocking hard.

What — we have become
friends? Not so bad,
not so good. Tonight, tomorrow,

you stare from your city window
into the white others, suddenly stunned
by the numbers of them, by number
itself. These days

I stand in my garden of weeds,
telling the corn that's not there
how tall it has grown, praising
invisible beans.

When we meet
we meet in the middle.
We inch halfway across the floor, so far!
No farther.

After the years — what?
We can tell each other *things:*
branches and thickets, streets, lovers gone or returning,
low times, low moons in the morning.
My friend, what

do we know?
Perhaps all our talk just makes things worse
by making it easier for us to assume

that after the years we are friends,
intimate ones. What do we know?
We spill a few dust motes
into a room, then turn,

still wearing our sheets, holes
cut out at the eyes, carrying old bags and boarding

our different trains
with all of their windows,
with all of the other ghosts.

It's a postcard,
a picture of sun as sphincter — far
from correct. There's a place
missing, a pain
so bored with its story
it packed a duffel and wandered off. Like you,

the postcard was innocent. Like you
it was gesture, fingers
closing into their palms, saying:
Be sorry for me! Be sorry. But
that's one of the problems
with gesture, liable

to many interpretations.
And with postcards, picturesque
derisions of this planet,
the footprints of a lover
avoiding himself. Somehow that
was the point you missed. Sometimes

there was nowhere to look
not already dark. So: the sun closes,
pulls the sky shut around it. It's like you:
a man always crossing the threshold backwards,
a man disappearing
into a hole which is also

disappearing.
I receive your postcard.
You've become what you always wanted:
to be beyond
the thermometer's burning, beyond the zero.

32 ☙ *Eben*

(1956–1979)

If Eben could do it
we can. It's certain
we can't go on like this, not
belonging. We don't have flags
tied to our wrists. We aren't even aware
that way under the grass
water, whales are screaming.
Eben took the phone off the hook,
locked the door
and did it.
In a single motion the chair
spilled over and a silence
moved in
and out of that room
for three days.

This is not
a lucky place to be.
We could put our heads
together. We could reinvent
the ways. We could even decide:
let's all get
Eben. Let's clobber that dead boy
till he calls out what he knew all along:
that pain is green,
that we stand on the lawn days
looking for it and never realize

the grass is the camouflage.
And way under
the whales sing — *oi weih*, way
under.

The people I don't know
want to talk about your suicide.
They say the word like an old barn roof
drooping into its own weight,
like a day all beak and feather – no bird.
They don't like

being startled the way you startled them
so they call it your *departure*
and put it in a hallway
where no scars are kept.
Just a suitcase
and they don't have to think

that suitcase is empty;
they don't have to think
of a scar pinned to your wrists
like an orchid.

The people I don't know
say the word *suicide* like an empty jugular,
like a towhee soaring
into glass. But I say

it's simple, just what we take
by pointing away from ourselves.
Something like diving precisely
into the moon
on a lake: the downgrace
of an eyelash, water seeming to bend
the long stick of the spine.

The people I don't know
hear that word like nails being driven into a bucket.
I hear it like rain,

like my own outer heart on the roof
as you're walking away,
walking off with yourself—
no message, just elsewhere.

As in the portrait of the girl on the beach
that hangs across from the man with the gold chain
dangling from his fob, you are left to look on
an elegance already beyond issue.
All these paintings are of your family
though you say *family* as if something has splintered
your tongue.

*   *   *

I remember the way we both stood
in front of that church in Ponce
neither leaving the door
nor going inside and you
saying there was no Father, that the Father
was dead — I thought suddenly
it wasn't guilt
but innocence that kept you outside.
Still there is something in you that wants Him
the way you want your own father back.

*   *   *

I'm not driving
at anything particular here, not saying *vittima, povera,*
for some there are arrivals
for some, departures. I'd almost be sorry
if everything did make sense. You've simply learned
when things are taken away
to look in the direction in which they went. What else
were you supposed to do
in Ponce? Knowing
you were innocent, knowing
you'd have to pay for it.

Today snow
trying to get into the house
waters
at the doorjamb. It's a wish
become too accurate, wish
at work against itself. All that I wanted

resumes its banging
like a tin spoon on my forehead.
Desire holds me here. I forget
that it costs, forget
how much of what is gotten
is gotten by excluding others. Today,

snow. I know it will stop soon. I believe
it can't. The flakes are driven
against the window screen, constant repetitions
of the sound of failure, birds

breaking open their lives
on sheet glass, my own fallen people equally
broken, my own little men and women thirsty
from exorbitance. How much

more than what I wanted
have I asked and organized,
arbitrating letters of my life
until I'm here,
carried by desire into the snows of this
particular winter. I'm alone.
I would have preferred to be anything else
but what I am,
what I wanted to be
so badly.

FOR RANDALL JARRELL, 1914–1965

The simple fact that you were an artist
would have amused you since,
of all your admirers, you
were the least. Other facts:
how you were harried,
how you walked
from the canvas to the window —
again, again — drawing the colors out
as if from the perfect earth itself.
There could be consummations and the painting
become a work of the day laborer
who carries clay up from the riverbank.
Back and forth he moves with the yoked buckets
full of sienna until the last muscle
is spent. The painting arises finally
out of a kind of weariness,
the body having traveled long
between its sources.
You came to yourself so late, saying *I am the artist*,
being already seated by the river
and having set the yoke down
like a gift.

There is absence enough to last a lifetime
had we sense of lifetime.
Again and again love lifts its arms wanting
to be indicted among us —
but those arms, and the children of those arms!
It seems we can't say it enough, goodbying
our miles, shaking hands
as if we were swimmers stroking water.

How many abstractions come down to the water
standing in a clear vase cut
with stem. This is the measuring of our ardor,
how we perpetuate the image of love
by making murder last
and last. See how the flowers lean
on one another the way our arms
depend from the heart.
Ships mill
about harbor waiting for the word:
Avast! Avast…

Ave. Ave:
words said in welcome.
Or farewell. The traitor the tongue is,
our mind's changeable hostess,
which also dwells in water, liable
to refraction as everything bends
under the tonnage of goodbye.
What disservice we do ourselves. In the eye's waterlight,
the world goes ocher. *Forever*
is a word we can't use. We leave off
before all beginnings, saying *So much*
has already gone by the boards, saying *Enough*
of absence. Enough.

I remember waving a close friend off
from the station; my arms kept up
their ignoble flapping even after
the train had gone. Sometimes
I think my life is just that:
hands
hung in the air a moment too long. Love's so much

a departure, friendship turned
to its second face, as if presence itself
could turn to its absence. Oh,
but we pluck our meanings
out of air, making things count
and counting them, so many prayers
told on a single bead.

My friend's gone
to the other end of this country —
and, it's funny, I'm here
marketing my particular stillness. Emotions
are semi-nomadic. But the bones,
our bones, they're able to house
these frangible moments.

Sometimes the days fall like coats
we strip from ourselves. We get closer
to something, some
sacristy love
has shaped by our love. Say we're all
just goodbyes of ourselves —
we've said what matters.
Our lives are like fingers spread in the air
long after the train
has gone.

1.
To think of this planet as
planet, and to assume
nothing. The soul suffers apartheid, knows it
and waits in the anteroom
for the body to summon it forth, provide
the trajectory.

If I could only believe
in the conditional tense!
If there were even that much
collaboration between cause and effect –
the evidence is overwhelming
ambivalence, every direction
the right one to take considering
we are expected nowhere

under the wide nacre sky. I feel insular,
an evolutionary mistake,
as if *Homo sapiens* were a categorical
blunder, *or* as if I were in this alone.
Are we in this alone? Planet,
there's no embracing you. There's no embracing
fortuity at all. Therefore
we ignore it. The soul insists
on design, thinks it can slough off the body.
Soul – that's nomenclature. Soul,
subclassification falling under
Breastbone, the.

2.
It's true, our tragedies
are distant, things we once felt
about thinking.
Here on earth we can travel far

from earth. I once spent an hour
holding a chip of glass to light,
turning it under my thumb
like a solid tear, sorrow perceived.

My friend? *Friends* —
could words make us that,
could words insist
on their meaning?
(This morning the pervasive dream.
I wait on an airfield for my family to arrive.
Their plane skids in, its large shoulders
swooping down, bound back by air to earth.
But no one disembarks.
I don't see anyone
disembark. Then
I am awake having this dream.)

3.
Rilke says departure's
the human condition. Paul says
the good we would do,

the good…can we be responsible
for our natures and not
for the natural condition? Christ
made death abashed, you see, but He
was Christ and I can't stop goodbyes
from fumbling past my lips, oh goodbye then,
goodbye…

4.
At the last
it's easier to be abstract.
We all burn for our heavens,

burn irresolute while the planet
hurtles on, holding its place
in some tertiary constellation. We are seen
from afar, oh then we are

afar,
for this is the planet
where separation
is gravity, separation
the volatile force. Finally
it's meaning
that insists on words. Like solar flowers
we are made to *open*
and so we open
here. For a time.

It is always James. It is
James again and again
because of some accident
at birth, because occasionally the great evening sky
slumps over the pines it is
James.

In the small nape of his life we tried to touch
back to infancy so often
thinking it was a kind of bridge for him, for us — as if,
being wrongly made, he would stay forever
young enough for us to explain, *It happens
to children, it isn't
James's fault*. There are useless waters
covered with a delicate ice which welcome
James and we half hope, we half
hope…

Still, it is James again, late afternoon leaning
towards a clear day tomorrow and James wants
to come with me to the station, to meet "Daddy," "for Daddy"
he stands on the platform waiting
as James himself, the boy I can't
explain anymore — there
with hands stuffed in his tall pockets
in the dusk of fathers traveling home
towards lightly floured wives
who open icebox doors. I imagine the men traveling
are tired and the women leave sticks
of butter to soften on the counter….Oh James

we don't really
wish you those waters, it's just this hour

when the familiar becomes
grotesque because it is
so familiar and because
it is you James
standing in these last lights
where you will always stand,
a form
before darkness, before night.

FOR EVA

There was a beautiful poet
and a line of his came back to you
at your father's funeral, so that when you bent
over the half-opened casket you said, "Thank you,
thank you. You have broken
into blossom, you have broken

into blossom."
You asked me to stay with you that night
and from the couch I could hear you
crying and crying. There was nothing
I could do and I guess that's why I wanted
to take you by the hand or maybe
by the bones in your shoulder and tell you
"Save it." *Save it.*

It would have been cruel.

   * * *

I am cruel sometimes and deal
in starved abstractions. How will you look back
on this year? Is the universe
getting smaller? How much worse
is it going to get, Eva, how much
worse and are you trying
to be ready?

   * * *

Standing here
in this ingenious dusk
there is something
I want to rescue. I want to believe

something can be rescued. But is
death such an orchestra? Do we
blossom when we break? Since your father died
I've been afraid to ask you.

But let's say
yes, let's say *yes something*
can be saved, maybe just this
dusk, the sun's parachuting
into the trees, the corn-yellow beak
of a blackbird flying so slowly and patiently,
a dark thing rowing
into the dark.

It is the simplest of things.
Today.
To die by doing so.

His voice comes back to me.
It is my body reopened.
He says, *I was born into the wrong world,*
now I am in this other,
this other where I belong,
and you, also…

I hold his photograph to candlelight, meaning
it to burn. In the play of light
I can make his lips move, or
I can let the candle speak first.

Yes, this time I want the candle
to speak first, turning
the whole house to flame, room after room

cleaned of its burden
while I prepare for sleep; such a simple thing!
Closing the bedroom door,
the fire insisting, *this other, this other…*
Closing. By doing so.

THREE

I love the ladders of a poem
and the sudden aging of my own hands
as I'm limping away, miserable, addle-brained,
delighted. As much as your face! A rouse!
For your face that I've never touched
but wanted to. I've wanted to put three fingers
to the balcony of your cheek,
to close the wet lips of your eye.

For all this, I still
love like a woman who's afraid
loves. I have such frightened hands
I can't help wrestling with them.
I can't help it when they tear
pages out of the book,
mad as angels.

I may be vanishing.
I may be the girl who wasn't.
Oh, but these breasts seem
actual and the longing so airless,
the bones beautiful, bright as shells.
Such a redolent, smiling
impoverishment. Love
makes me turn back, animal-heavy, stars
budding under my collar.
I'm turning back to the point where I'm almost
balancing, almost enhaloed
as the ladders are being drawn up.

Rain draws
its stupid face on the window. Your letters
come like a hammer-tap
to the knee.
   Please,

please don't write me anymore.
We live by such simple implements:
knife, spoon, hacksaw, longing
that will be here forever,
     please.

Let's not compare notes, but be something
in an ocher-lit painting, facsimile
of lovers in a field, fulfilled.
Sundown or sunrise: the man reads a book, the woman

is making a nest of daisies.
In sunrise, the man looks up, sees
the woman, in sunset
in tears in a painting
with tears on her face.

I think of you
out of some excruciate memory
of a kiss wholly taken.
Meaning can drift for miles
and still be broken into coins
for you, a party horn
you blow and blow.

Here, everything is founded on the principle
that the past recedes, that memory
can be stroked and taught to purr.
So even this loneliness
is a bluff, a vast hovering
that is not a true distance.

Oh mine, mine! Words
that limp a little and balk in mid-road.
Love was obdurate that way, refusing every
final possession. But still, that kiss —
it was taken from me, *taken*.
Though I know you'll make a meaning

that suits the next occasion, her
longer and light hair
fanned on the pillow slip, you
staring down at her…
Here it will be gradual,
this letting go, gradual

though somewhere in the future
there is already a day
when the kiss is something afforded, a copper
for you to put in your box, a letter that comes
to mean nothing, that is just
a kiss, what is expended, what is spared.

I've been reading your love poems
but they bore me. Married men
bore me. Any man with his woman
bores me.

All day I stood just
out of the watermark.
The dolphins occupied me —
even if they do mean
bad weather — they *occupied* me.
(I wanted you here, not
saying anything.)

Pelicans don't
bore me at all. I can hear them
in their almost voiceless flying,
in their stretched V's, wings
not touching. I think probably you
are touching a woman now.
I think I could never tell you
the approaches of salt, the extent
of the watermark.

But suppose the night's easier. Suppose
this beach a night and these boats bridges.
I could cross over.
I could leave my shoes on the railing and become
indefinitely vanished.

I wanted to be in
your love poems, but I was missing
as if half a life were missing.
But, after all, it isn't.
It's just timid of light years.
It's just waiting out the day and losing itself

in the white foam spilling
over the dolphin's back, way out there
in waves we'll never inhabit.

always arrives from a third source.
Is it that this is the world
of triads and triplicates?

When I try to imagine your pain
there's no bridge to it.
The way this rain bottles the air

makes breathing a skill.
How can I acquire
the great emphatic lungs of listening?

*News of you, news
of you*. Nearby an entire grove
must lift into sky, a bird huddle tight

under its wet wing. What comfort
is there?
With its factualness and its mystery

news comes like certain habitual clues: the umbrella
gone from its stand, a voice on the phone saying, "Oh,
but I thought you knew."

*   *   *

Did you know
I once wanted to be your wife?
And now that she

has really left you I'm touched
by the profanity of what I wanted.
How will you do

without her? Certainly the heart
will gather its anthologies, dazed pieces
that add up to nothing

cognitive. And then
will come the shouldering
of the real grief:

the anger
that slaps like mad fish on the deck
shattering scales everywhere until it's all

silver,
the metallic petaling
of rage duffed in tears.

*   *   *

I have heard from someone,
heard you lost the half of you
you loved more easily. And I

am in my halves as well.
The past courses between us like a third element,
her name, her story telling itself

in the language of deft water
that carves us
far into distances.

There's no bridge
to you from here,
no bridge or boat. Boat,

how I loved you! Boat
that isn't there.

What was it
that made you bring tulips
the night before
you left? Each docile head
cut from the skin of a perfect thigh,
what a punishment
of beauty…

Today towards noon
my neighbor's granddaughter
leads me with child-seriousness
into her yard. We stand together
in front of a young willow tree.
"It is so beautiful," she says,
"they call it 'weeping.'"

I said thank you for the tulips
and placed them carefully,
up to their necks
in water. And how I wept that night,
how I wept to punish you.

You are not a dead man
but I remember you with that
kind of closure.
Like the felled hickory
becoming so helplessly comprehensible
you seem suddenly
precarious, even petulant —
if I must pity what I've admired
I should prefer not to admire. You see,

I want to talk about you in a very
past tense. I want to say, "Oh, him?"
I want to say, "Yes, he was
a quiet man." I'd like to invent the story of your life
as if it *were* story, a silent film
in which she kisses him and the subtitle reads
"They kiss." In fact, that
above all, that when they kiss
the mind abstracts itself because it *has* to,
because I can't go on

unless my heart is instructed to go on
and has its instructions properly memorized....
Because I love you, because I'm afraid
to love you, because I don't
want this love to die I must kill for you.
I must say, "Heart,
this is the end. Heart,
this is the only way to go on."

I play "Turtle Dear" on the piano
because it's the only song I know.
The house is audible,
the way the world works. It outsings
the heart; wall
meets wall, corners
are law.

I play for a long while
the same notes, "Said Turtle Dear
to Turtle Dark," over and over. Later
there will be time to put on lamps. Later
I will spread light liberally
and the house will gleam. Light will soften edges
of the highboy and fall yellow
across our bed, there will be some comfort there.

Today noonlight
made the street unnaturally white.
I bought coffee. On another street
I bought more coffee. I don't think
your absence is fatal, though I was anxious all day
to get home. Now
I am home. I touch

every possible object
we have touched. Things feel covered
with a kind of light dust, the sheen
of grit on a traveler's lip. And there is the highboy,
saying that its sadness is practiced, saying
that we live in an obedience
of walls.

There is no backdrop, no reason
for us to be lovers. Love insists
but is never the reason
we turn
or stay. In this orchard
ladders gather no shadow, no pretext
for the skies
which do what they've been told to do,
what they've practiced doing
since they were skies. I get carried away
by a remorse for these ladders. I've always been intimate
with them, but tonight
I'm carried away with their ease,
with the disdainful way I've left them in the orchard
without turning back, without
holding them one more time…the pale trees
pale, the ladders
that have always been my entry
into sky.
Tonight I give them up. Tonight?
No backdrop. No reason.

I have just come to accept
my acceptance, your
wishing me to live beyond
those fixed terminologies
of affection usually set by parents
for runaways. In my blood,
no more coffins swim, no
settees with my mother's heels hiding beneath.
Simple blood
runs and gathers, congeals
as it should so that at night I begin
to dream fluently
of words: *stamina.*
Hieratic. I dream
of the baton being handed from the sweating relay runner
to the tense, unbreathing second. I become
the runner, the one
about to lose or win. The thought
doesn't scare me as it once did. *Sacristy.*
Meccas. Words I dream and have to look up
in the morning so that like an illiterate
or somnambulist I falter
through the dictionary to see
what possible meanings
gratitude might hold. Runaways
and brides are similar
despite their mixed fortunes. One can even
become the other, so that in kissing
your hand to leave, I kiss your hand
and stay. As I am about to run off
I realize I have finished with running, am white

with joy. I throw down the baton, say
"Damn you, I'll stay, damn
you," swearing like this
out of habit,
out of love.

happening in me at that time.
And now, memory
ascending memory, the grained catalpa leaf
on water, the acacia,
thrombosis of the past.

Traveling back
to the things I hoped never to see again
I come up hard
against you, the dull thud
of sex and, afterwards, that childish ambition
towards romance – bodies made simple
with fatigue, memory
being cleaned like a knife.

Still, the eye grows thick
with what it has seen.
Time delays itself
with the rubrics of nostalgia. And then,
there is again only the sweet catalpa
floating downriver, and the acacia
grown wild against your back porch
like the heart
against the fence of the body.

Dearheart,
        Stoneheart,
I have touched your face among branches
and come back from the woods thinking
that touch is the banishing
of what we touch — how I turned from you
from wanting you.

This is a poor excuse
in defense of the mirage
that backed off into itself, an excuse
that vitiates love
for the sake of the unhappiness
it turns out to be. Hanging shirts
to dry in the backyard I reprove
the weapon I've become to myself, imagining
our love both possible and not, a thing gone forward
into its end;
what was unavoidable, met. A cardinal
comes to the ilex,
a red so brilliant as to be red

beyond recall.
Then, how he's suddenly gone
though for a second I still see him there,
a bit of ribbon, a kiss thrown
to the bush.
Between the possible and the real
there is such flourishing of hope.

But the goodbye in every greeting, every entreaty
we made towards one another, facts that are hybrids
and principalities that point

not to happiness, or to grief
but to the both-sidedness

of what we were: lives
that couldn't merge or yield
to each other more than
the grim going on that is
both departure and staying behind,
a red in the still air rising, a song
that by the window descends.

FOR T.

I will begin by saying *nevertheless*
as scholars say *nevertheless.*
Only I'm not a scholar so when I say it I mean
nevertheless love as in
nevertheless when you lay your dusty head down
in the greater dust of earth
the dust won't be as simple as you thought; the dust
is not even dust and you will not sleep. Oh, sleep —
sleep and the voices of sleep
that call to us both, only call us away,

always away. Should we come back
to that ancient theme? Is it worth coming back to?
My hands are tired of talk and words.
They're big as the willows, they want to fill seas. But for you
they retract, for you they sway, awkward as gavels,
bumping into lamps, knocking over glasses of water, saying
lamps, glasses of water, trying to keep away
from the one word that might
frighten us both, suddenly, finally:
possible. Possible love
is not always murder.

But we go on, watching ourselves meet
in the distance, crossing
like branches, like boats — you
so sure of the end
that it won't let you begin; and me,
insisting against you, hearing only
some other voice strongly calling me now.
Possible. Possible. I end
this letter as I began, without your help,

in no shape to give or retrieve the words
and with no right to be blessed, or to bless —
as I do now, nevertheless, as I bless you.

Somehow the unexpected does
occur, and we mourn
until we are nothing but pure again, ready
for this world to do us in or,
perhaps, to turn for a day
without touching us, without afflicting
the merest acquaintance. It's been a long
week, a longer
day, and we are tired
enough to mention only
the trivial: how snow
kept most people from coming; if the service
was too long. If anything
it was too short and neither of us
cried, not before
or during, until we wondered
if we were crippled in the heart. But tonight
it happens. I cry
because I can't get the zipper
on my briefcase to work; you,
because it keeps on snowing
and being winter all the time. Some days
it's good to say what we don't mean,
to just lie down and be exhausted.

You say the snow makes you think
of swans, so I think
of those birds too, and of any bird
in nighttime with her bones of air, flesh
of feather. It's like nothing
or to be made into nothing, this whitest
grief, this flight
in the body.

As it grows
towards winter, I begin
the systematic killing. I start with ferns,
the overbearing spider
plants that have been moved
indoors and seem
to hang everywhere. There is no
headroom in this glass
weight of my own
doing. After the plants, the snow
is free to shake down.

I like the regular weather inside
this domed marriage. Months
have risen, fallen
like water. I get more
plastic by day, even to myself, feeling
from within I feel only
the object I'm becoming, willfully
insular, as the murderer must somehow be
held apart, less
for what he has done
than for what he knows
he has done. *Betrothal,*
a word so near to *betrayal,* our ears
have tricked our hearts. I hold

my face. I stand by the flat church.
I am shaken terribly, and remotely
some more familiar life floats down. Snow,
an old way of being, my skin
like isinglass now
from the killing, from standing unreachably
close to these narthex doors, to you
whom I love, to the slim

blue sky above me from which
comes the distance, false
as it is
absolute.

I've watched you
in the way of one whose life is dissembled
by what she has chosen
to notice.
You say, "Times of isolation
are over." But how do I know
if the leaves pinwheeled to my heart
are leaves light has touched?
As we've never touched, never
will touch…

Some days we must deal in facts.
Some days we get on
with our living that's really a spilling
of what we imagine: the marriage of impossible
orchids, a passage
from *verging* to *burgeon*
that never takes place.
My hands are two intimates
walking apart; your fingers, tremulous
stamen and pistil
waving in every possible gesture – above all
in goodbye. Flowers will do that.
But flowers will do.

So I watch you and I'm all
forgiveness. I forgive you and the orchids
because you've done nothing. I forgive even
my life
that's the simplest
water jar
standing on a bureau wondering

if it's there to hold flowers
or if it has,
has held them already.

Do you know, I don't think
the isolation is
over. Do you know, I think it has
held flowers already.